The Universe You Swallowed Whole

poems by

Scott Hughes

Finishing Line Press
Georgetown, Kentucky

The Universe You Swallowed Whole

For Sara,
i carry your heart with me

Copyright © 2020 by Scott Hughes
ISBN 978-1-64662-154-5 First Edition
All rights reserved under International and Pan-American Copyright Conventions. No part of this book may be reproduced in any manner whatsoever without written permission from the publisher, except in the case of brief quotations embodied in critical articles and reviews.

ACKNOWLEDGMENTS

I must thank the editors of the publications in which these poems first appeared:

armarolla ~~"Alternative Facts" and "Math after Mandelbrot"
Chiaroscuro ~~"Ode to Nothing"
Former People ~~"The Breathing Dark," "Charon's Obol," "For Anya—August 6, 2018," "For My Child, Who Will Never Exist," "Ghosts," "Scaled Harmonics," "The Wind of We," and "Workshop Poem"
Humanagerie ~~"Pray"
Minute Magazine ~~"Two Wrens Sleeping"
One Sentence Poems ~~"Death of a Song," "Old Plot," "Schrödinger's Rejection Letter," "Visitation," and "Will"
Rat's Ass Review ~~"Beginning at the End of Things," "Sisters, Perennial," and "To Robert Frost, You Bastard"
Redheaded Stepchild ~~"5/4"
Strange Horizons ~~"Swans Take Flight at My Father's Grave"

Many writers learn and practice their craft under the mentorship of great teachers. I have been lucky enough to learn from some of the best poets: Susan Atefat Peckham, Gordon Johnston, Martin Lammon, Judson Mitcham, and Anya Silver. My undying gratitude goes to my family as well; they have encouraged me to write poems and stories since I first learned the alphabet.

Publisher: Leah Maines
Editor: Christen Kincaid
Cover Art: *Aurora*, by Jamey Grimes, www.jameygrimessculpture.com
Author Photo: Sara Pirkle Hughes
Cover Design: Elizabeth Maines McCleavy

Printed in the USA on acid-free paper.
Order online: www.finishinglinepress.com
      also available on amazon.com

Author inquiries and mail orders:
Finishing Line Press
P. O. Box 1626
Georgetown, Kentucky 40324
U. S. A.

Table of Contents

I. All Poets Are Liars
Litany for a Poet and an Audience 2
Workshop Poem 3
Schrödinger's Rejection Letter 4
Alternative Facts 5
To Robert Frost, You Bastard 6

II. Such Beautiful Suffering
The Wind of We 8
Sisters, Perennial 9
Scaled Harmonics 10
Math after Mandelbrot 11
Two Wrens Sleeping 12
Pray 13
The Night, She Sings 14

III. Words Are Stones
The Breathing Dark 16
My Father's Lips 17
Old Plot 18
Visitation 19
Ghosts 20
5/4 21
Beginning at the End of Things 22

IV. The Waters of Dreamless Nothing
For Anya—August 6, 2018 24
Ode to Nothing 25
Death of a Song 26
Swans Take Flight at My Father's Grave 27
Charon's Obol 28
Will 29
For My Child, Who Will Never Exist 30
What Sweet Sleep 31
This Path Worn 32

I. All Poets Are Liars

Litany for a Poet and an Audience

As a poet, I promise to offer no sappy love poems,
no poems about the majestic flight of the crane,
no poems about God's design in turtle shells,
no poems about finding peace in death.

> *As an audience, we promise to hang*
> *onto your every word, laugh when we*
> *should laugh, cry when we should cry.*

I promise to challenge your thoughts
and help you to see things differently.
I promise to keep your interest.

> *We promise not to fall asleep*
> *or nod our heads and pretend to listen.*
> *We are open ears. We are open minds.*

As a poet, I promise you will love everything
I have written. My words will pour from my mouth,
and you will soak them up like desert sand.

> *We know that poets do not speak* the *truth,*
> *only* their *truth. We know that all poets are liars,*
> *but we promise to believe you.*

Workshop Poem

This is not a poem
about your stupid cat
or your grandmother's hands
or the small of your lover's back,
not the pomegranate you savored
or the decadent marzipan
you bought in Florence
or that poem you wrote
just to use the word *marzipan*,
not the time you got high
or all those other times you got high
or that meaningful exchange
you had with the homeless man,
not the mountain you climbed
or the ocean you swam
or the universe you swallowed whole
like a goddamn ping pong ball.

Schrödinger's Rejection Letter

When I find a new email
in my inbox from a journal

I submitted to, I wait to open it
because in that moment

my writing is simultaneously
rejected and accepted.

Alternative Facts

In 1966, when man first conquered the moon,
the last atomic bomb was disassembled
by Soviet scientists with help from aliens
from Jupiter's moon Io. The Ionians
then bestowed the gift of foresight to humankind,
which we used to create the first time machine
that had actually already been created
in order to travel back to 1966 to instruct us
how to construct it. Don't try to figure out
the logistics of time travel: that's what the Ionians
want us to do, to busy ourselves with conundrums
while they use our moon to alter Earth's gravity.
Have you noticed lately how light you feel
with each step you take? How, with maybe just
a strong enough leap, you could launch yourself
high enough into the stratosphere to see
the entire artic wall that rings our flat planet?

To Robert Frost, You Bastard

Whose words these are I think I know.
Your lines are on my bookshelf though;
You cannot stop me writing here,
Just watch your words be copied so.

My little pen must think it queer
To stop without an end rhyme… close.
Between semesters—summer break—
My only writing time each year.

I give my aching wrist a shake
And tell myself I'm not a fake,
Plagiarist, literary sheep.
Not everyone is William Blake.

Your words are lovely, dark and deep,
But I have delusions to keep,
And lines to go before I sleep,
And lines to go before I sleep.

II. Such Beautiful Suffering

The Wind of We

For a moment, forget
the force that holds us
together, that binds
our atoms one to another
and keeps them
from flying apart
into a cloud of ourselves
that the next passing breeze
might waft away, dispersing
the microscopic homogeny
of you and me and them
across the globe.

Sisters, Perennial

Spring mourns, ignoring the saplings
and blossoms sprouting from her fallen tears,
and tells the rotted trees and wilted flowers:

Summer caresses the ripe fruit, rolls
it across her breasts and thighs, kisses
its crimson skin, and whispers:

Autumn torments the trees she touches,
yet they submit, offering her their leaves—brittle browns,
carnal reds, candlelight yellows—as she murmurs:

Winter shrouds nature under her silver quilt,
pondering her sisters' work—Spring
grieving the earth abloom, Summer
promising each seed it will live forever, Autumn
bestowing such beautiful suffering—and as Winter
calls forth the first warm winds, she sings:

Scaled Harmonics

Scaled harmonics: lens of electron microscope: Jesus on crucifix.
We delve deep with these tools into the pulsing nexus
of the universe, the atom, the purest tone, the church, ourselves.
Particles in constant vibration. A remote star flickers and implodes

We search for truth in Shakespeare.
We search for truth in concentric redwood rings.
We search for truth in the Flesh and the Blood and the Word.
We search for truth in heliotropes and isotopes.

We hope to hone the cosmos to a single note.
We hope to cup it in our hands as a seed.
We hope to peel back the layers to the core.
We hope to find God focused like a pin-prick of light.

Math after Mandelbrot

golden rectangle —
deity derived —
replicate (*infinite!*) inside
& beyond itself : fury in fractal —
radiate & center into pixels : blips : moons :
binary (faces of god —
faces of man) code :
1   0   0   1
luminous data construct —
endless repetitions cycle down
to zenith   —   *n*   —
become language : subtract
multiply   add
(*divine!*)   divide

Two Wrens Sleeping

Atop my porch window
I find them huddled together,
their heads hidden
and their synchronous breaths
like the pulses
of a single feathery heart.

Pray

Look, here in my palm as this praying mantis
turns its pyramid head. Keep your mouth
closed. It will count your teeth, and if it finishes,

you will die. Watch its legs, tapered to points.
Watch its spiny arms like broken tusks fold in prayer,
worshipping the chitinous god of stained-glass wings,

of exoskeletons, of antennae sensual as tongues
or fingertips. I raise it to my face to see if it will count
my teeth, numbering each one with its pointed spur.

I see my face captured in the inky dome of its eye.
Does it understand its own head mirrored in my pupil
as its forelegs conduct an arthropodal choir I cannot hear?

The Night, She Sings

Hear her music,
the dark's whisper
and insects' hymn
that can seem so lonely
but are there to hold you
in what life is:
                the moon's
motherly embrace
and the night's breath
against your skin,
reminding you that you
are both body
and more than body.

III. Words Are Stones

The Breathing Dark

You held me for a million million years
in boundless darkness without fear
before I was I and be was be,
before blinding sky and rocking sea,
before I knew you could disappear.

Your whisper breathed my body here.
Until you spoke, I had no ears,
no mind to fathom the mystery
held in you a million million years.

With closed eyes, I still felt you near,
though blistering sun began to sear
the vision you had gifted me.
Darkness is not what blind men see.
Our eyes burn with countless fiery spheres—
stars dying for a million million years.

My Father's Lips

I remember my father's plump lips, round
and soft like blankets. Briefly my dad pressed
them to my forehead and without a sound
checked for a fever, his palm on my chest.
His warm breath smelled of aged copper, my nose
scratched and tickled by stubble on his chin.
Heat passed from my head to his mouth. He chose
to take it from me, like lifting a sin
from me: God's dim whisper behind his face.

I cannot do the same for him now.
Silence hums in this cold room as I trace
curves of his hand with my forefinger. How
I want to reach my dad. I long to hold
my lips to his scalp, clean and slightly cold.

Old Plot

My father drives me around his new property,
a tract slicing into the Okefenokee Swamp,
and points out the grotesquely twisted pines,
the spot where a B-29 fireballed to earth in '48,
and the nearly toppling house where Seminoles
led by Billy Bowlegs slaughtered an entire family,
and he says, "One day this will be yours."

Visitation

My brother sits across from me
in the prison visiting room,
his jumpsuit the color
of coffee-stained teeth, and says,
"Keep the letters coming.
Whenever I read them, I'm free."

Ghosts

When you find me writing at my desk,
tell me the paper will not yellow over time.
Tell me the ink will not fade or run.
Say my words will curl in as a conch shell
gathering sand for cover on the ocean floor.

Later, when you see me sleeping, whisper
in my ear that words are stones, breaking
rings into the surface of our lake.
Tell me they are the boards I paralleled,
nailed flat to build a dock.

Place my fingertips on the side
of your neck. Tell me words are there.
When I dream, show me blue ink
shining on white pages. Show me its ghost
bleeding through the other side.

My lips are words in the morning as you trace
them with your finger. As I rise from sleep,
tell me how an empty, cupped hand
and a clenched fist can both mean hunger.
Tell me words can close the hand, open the fist.

Give me the empty room, the smooth tabletop,
the blank pages resting there. Forget
to show me the door's rusty hinges,
the glassy pebbles on the bank of our lake,
the words hidden in the whorls of my fingers.

5/4

        brubeck tiptoes through cool shadows
sewer pipes & night thoughts swish & whirlpool
you are a single open ear—not a mind—not a soul
        brubeck baptizes clefs in sixteens & sevens
        brubeck reveals the trinity in treble
sleep won't come tonight with brubeck laying hands
legato fingers reel in the timbre of your wounds
        brubeck : composer of the downbeat
        brubeck : breaker of the metronome
you were born to sleep—to jazz—to reawaken
remember : he hammered you from bebop
        brubeck ascends on a current of coda
remember : jazz is the great unequaled slumber
the great unequaled : each note a rite : remember :

Beginning at the End of Things

So it all comes down to this: Life begins
to dwindle—the heavens no longer turn.
The seas and clouds and thoughts refuse to churn,
and underfoot the earth has ceased to spin.

Our blood is suspended beneath our skin.
But the cosmos is none of our concern,
and it all comes down to this: Life begins
to dwindle, the heavens no longer turn.

The planet loses its pull on us—then,
like dying suns, our bodies ebb and burn,
becoming more than flesh, the mortal urn.
We travel—our essence boundless, golden.
So it all comes down to this: Life begins.

IV. The Waters of Dreamless Nothing

For Anya—August 6, 2018

Today you rise
not from sleep
but from this
consciousness
into something
more, and outside,
the clouds are still,
as though you
are holding
them in place
for me to see,
to remember
this moment,
to live in this
wondrous now.

Ode to Nothing

It is nowhere.
It is everywhere.
It is, and it isn't.

It is around itself
and inside itself.
It is next to me but isn't.

I like where it is, next to me,
beside me—but not really—
light years away. It scares me.

It has no color, unless you
count itself as its color, or unless
you count all colors at once.
It swallows us.

We swallow it in return.
We hold it inside,
although we really can't.
We create it every day
and destroy it every day,
although we really can't.

It is small, like you or me.
It is vast, like you or me,
although we really aren't.
But we really are. It is the same
now as it was then
and as it always will be.
It is responsible for everything,
even itself. We owe it our lives,
and it will take them.

I never could stop thinking of it as a child.
It would not let me go, although it really did.
You will not let it go, although you already have.

Death of a Song

As I drive,
a bird flies
under my tire,
and I feel
its bones shatter
and wonder
what songs
it was meant
to sing.

Swans Take Flight at My Father's Grave

I have to admit,
this poem is not about swans
or visiting the plot
where my father is buried.
In fact, he's still alive.
I said that so you
would read this:
there are no
such things as swans
or graves or fathers.
Only flight. Put down this poem,
see it now: the black hole
stretching like a mouth,
taking in houses, oceans,
planets. Open your eyes,
quicken past moons,
novae, nebulae, dying
suns. Let the vacuum
swallow you until
the surrounding light curves
so far into itself you see
the back of your body.

Charon's Obol

On Father's Day,
my dad buries
his own father,

tucks a penny
in his father's
stiff hand, and I

want to take
the coin to put
in my dad's hand

when he ends
this journey
and begins another.

Will

You died years ago,
but since you don't
have a gravesite, I find
myself still leaving you
messages on social media,
digital prayers that I hope
reach you through the code
of zeroes and ones.

For My Child, Who Will Never Exist

You will never know
the ache of ticking seconds,
of realizing certainty
doesn't exist except
for inevitable uncertainty,
of the dawning agony
that you are trapped
in slowly dying meat
waiting to become
the eternal radiance
you already are.

What Sweet Sleep

What sweet sleep will come
when oblivion cloaks me,
like plunging into a dark lake
on a summer night, where I'll join
everyone who came before me
in the waters of dreamless nothing
and await you, whom I will embrace
with arms warm as the blood flowing
now, but not always, in our veins.

This Path Worn

Take my hand,
and let us walk

this path worn
by other weary feet.

Let our silence fill
with all things unsaid

by those who
trod here before.

Bring us peace they never felt,
solace they never sought.

Speak your worst secrets,
and I will set them aflight

for the wind to whisk away.
Take again my hand,

and let us walk,
travelers almost home

with lighter loads to bear.

Scott Hughes is a Georgia writer who graduated from Mercer University and then received an MFA in creative writing from Georgia College & State University. His fiction, poetry, and essays have appeared in such publications as *Crazyhorse, One Sentence Poems, Entropy, Deep Magic, Carbon Culture Review, Redivider, Redheaded Stepchild, PopMatters, Strange Horizons, Odd Tales of Wonder,* and *Compaso: Journal of Comparative Research in Anthropology and Sociology*. His collection of horror short stories, *The Last Book You'll Ever Read*, is available from Sinister Stoat Press, an imprint of Weasel Press. *Horrors & Wonders*, his second short story collection, is forthcoming later this year. He is the Division Head of English at Central Georgia Technical College and is currently finishing a young adult novel, *Red Twin*. He lives in Macon, Georgia, with his dog Pip. For more information, visit www.writescott.com.

www.ingramcontent.com/pod-product-compliance
Lightning Source LLC
LaVergne TN
LVHW041509070426
835507LV00012B/1445